LUTHERAN CHRISTIANS AND THEIR BELIEFS

Jerry L. Schmalenberger, D.Min.

Edited by
Carol Walthall Schmalenberger

7541 / ISBN 0-89536-979-6

Table of Contents

A FOREWORD

Jerry L. Schmalenberger

This six-part booklet was first written for a television presentation while I served as Senior Pastor of St. John's Lutheran Church in Des Moines, Iowa.

It is a composite of the material I have used in New Member classes over the years.

Worded with inclusive language, it has an ecumenical view. These elements are certainly consistent with Lutheran theology and with my entire ministry.

It does not put down other denominations, but, rather, tries to give positive information and comparison with our brothers and sisters in the Christian family. Lutherans are presented as one of the many legitimate Christian denominations.

Still, Lutherans have a rich heritage along with their contributions to basic beliefs, which I have tried to illustrate and describe.

The booklet can best be understood by reading with your Bible in hand. Now, dig in.

Jerry L. Schmalenberger

Dedicated
to
St. John's Lutheran Church

AN EVANGELIST

This book is in memory of John Dwight Brewbaker, whom everyone at St. John's Lutheran Church in Des Moines lovingly called "Brew." He was born November 22, 1903, and grew up a Methodist. Brew became a member of St. John's Lutheran Church the fall of 1926 at the age of 23 years.

He married Isabel Marie Jansen, daughter of Mr. and Mrs. Theodore W. Jansen, on August 30, 1928. Dr. Frederick Weertz performed the ceremony in the old brick church that has now been replaced by a gray stone one.

Dwight worked with Ted Cutler, a good friend in the plumbing business, at Sixth and Keo next to St. John's church. During the Depression he moved to the A. Y. McDonald Manufacturing Company as a wholesale salesman. He was with them forty years. At retirement age he moved to the City Supply Corporation and continued for eleven years. Three years after that were spent with the Iowa Plumbing, until his death.

All this time Dwight was a very active member of St. John's. He coached a winning basketball team. He served a number of terms on the Church Council and worked hard always in the area of Evangelism.

Dwight Brewbaker was elected Elder of St. John's on January 26, 1969.

He was on the Evangelism Committee for twenty-five years, beginning under Dr. Weertz.

"Izzie" and "Brew" called on the unchurched in Des Moines and hosted new member classes all those years.

The Brewbakers faithfully greeted people at the door of St. John's, and were well-known by all those who attended worship.

Dwight died January 23, 1982, of a heart attack while entering Veterans Auditorium to watch a basketball game, which he so enjoyed his entire life.

The Church Council of St. John's and Isabel, his good wife, thought it very appropriate that this book, which will be used primarily for Outreach and Evangelism, be dedicated to this man, one of the fine saints of our congregation.

PART 1

Who Are the Lutherans?

We pastors are a lot like doctors or lawyers when it comes to describing our church. We often use words which are known only to us who are inside the family of believers. For this reason, I would like to take time to tell you of the Christian church, using ten terms. We will consider these words one at a time to see how they describe what the Christian church is like and claims to be, and then apply them specifically to us Lutheran Christians.

The first word is *apostolic*. This means that the origin of our church is in the apostles and their traditions, practices, and faith statements.

An apostle was a person who actually lived at the time Jesus lived on earth and saw him face-to-face. After he was resurrected and ascended, the apostles had a special place in the whole structure of the Christian church. Because they had heard him speak and known him face-to-face, they were given considerable authority in the early church.

Now we take these worship practices of the apostles, their statements of belief, and the way they practiced their Christianity out in the world, as a very important guide for us in our day.

> **10 Great Words**
> Apostolic
> Evangelical
> Biblical
> Sacramental
> Confessional
> Catholic
> Ecumenical
> Liturgical
> Congregational
> Historical

Often you will hear things that we do in the Lutheran church called "apostolic." That simply means that we are trying our best to be consistent with the way the earliest Christians practiced their faith. We put special emphasis on those who saw Jesus face-to-face.

The second word is *evangelical*. This means that we aggressively share the Good News and invite others. It means that one of the primary responsibilities of a Lutheran Christian is to

> We are evangelical

invite unchurched people to be baptized and to become a part of the family of believers. This is intentional on our part. We don't just sit back and wait for people to ask to join like a lodge or other organizations you know in our day.

We see it as the responsibility of every member of the congregation to be an evangelist. We see the news that Christ has died and come out of the grave for us as extremely important, not only to the future lives of other people, but to the way they live right now. For this reason, our life is one of inviting.

We also include all sorts and kinds of people. We believe that the congregation must be inclusive: to invite and accept with open arms the rich, the poor, minorities and majorities — all sorts of ethnic backgrounds and educational levels.

Our belief about God is called a "theology of the cross." We do not hammer away at people with questions like, "Are you saved, brother?" Instead, we invite people to join us around the foot of the cross and enjoy the forgiveness that comes from it, which we all need.

Theology of:	
Cross	**Glory**
Forgiveness	Are you saved?
I'm also a sinner.	Is your soul okay?
We have help now.	Where will you spend eternity?

We never look down on other persons because they have not had the spiritual experience that we have. We see salvation as a gift from God to undeserving people. Our emphasis is as much on living this life right now as a Christian as it is on the joy of knowing that we are saved for eternity.

So, not only are we apostolic, but we are also evangelical, and that means we're inviting all people to join us.

The third word is *biblical*. This means that the basis of all our beliefs is the Bible. It is the final authority for all we do.

We are biblical

At the time of the Reformation, Martin Luther led quite a battle for this principle. The majority of Christians back in the 16th century felt that the Church was the final authority and only the Church had the knowledge to say what the Bible meant. It is solid Lutheran belief that a lay person or pastor, well-versed in the Scripture, is better equipped to live the Christian life from that basis than any other way.

You will notice that Lutheran Christians are continually talking about the Spirit and the revelations of the Scriptures as they set out what our behavior ought to be in our day.

We are not "biblical literalists." That is, we don't insist that the Bible dropped from heaven to us in its King James version.

We do not worship the Bible, but, rather, the Christ whom it reveals. We see the book as written by inspired people, but still humans, who were subject to error. For this reason, we always take the Scripture in its entirety, and we always interpret one verse in the light of others.

We Lutheran Christians are a biblical people. We study God's word, we teach God's word throughout all of our parish education programs, and we try to follow his word in our practice of ethics in the world.

We are biblical, we are evangelical, and we are apostolic.

We are also *sacramental*. At the time of the Reformation in the 16th century, a time of renewed interest and emphasis on the Scripture, three tests were set up to decide which would be the sacraments in the new reformed church: the

| We are sacramental |

act needed to be commanded by Scripture; there needed to be a promise connected with carrying out the sacrament; and there needed to be included an earthly element that people could actually see.

For these reasons, we Lutheran Christians have only two sacraments in our Church. Baptism is the way God adopts us into his family and gives us our second birth. Communion is the second sacrament and is the celebration of our membership in his family and his real presence with us now.

| Baptism as sacrament Communion as sacrament |

We believe that a sacrament is something God does to and for us. We also have rites that we practice in the church, such as marriage, burial of the dead, confession, ordination of pastors, confirmation.

We are sacramental because the main emphasis of our worship experience, practice, and outreach into the community, is on baptism, the way God adopts us into the family, and on communion, the way we gather and celebrate his presence with us now.

Sacramental, biblical, evangelical, and apostolic. We now look at the fifth word:

Confessional. This simply means that we have written documents which state what we believe, and we hold them to be very important. As we've said earlier, the Bible is the first and foremost document that reveals what we believe.

| We are confessional |

In addition to that, we have three creeds, a couple catechisms, and a primary document, called the Augusburg Confession, which was written in 1530.

All of these statements, written by human beings, are included in a book which we call the Book of Concord. They help us hand down from one generation to the next what Lutheran Christians have believed over the years.

| Book of Concord |

At the time of the Reformation in the 16th century, Martin Luther found that his priests and and many of his lay people were ignorant about the faith. He wrote a catechism, large flash

| Catechism |

cards which explained the Lord's Prayer, Apostles' Creed, and Ten Commandments. It was to be used by fathers around the meal table to teach their young people what Lutherans held as right and correct regarding God.

We still hold those teachings important, and our seventh, eighth, and ninth graders are taught from this same catechism before they are confirmed as adults in our church at the end of ninth grade.

In our worship service we use the Nicene and Apostles' Creeds. The Apostles' Creed is simply three answers to three questions that are asked of people when they are baptized. The Nicene Creed, which we use at communion services, is a

Creeds

little longer, and states what we hold in common with other Christians around the world.

The Augsburg Confession was written in 1530 when the Turkish army was about to invade Germany, and the Roman Catholics and Lutherans got together to see what they held in common. For that reason, it is an important document both to us and to the Roman Catholics as

Augsburg Confession

we work diligently to become brothers and sisters in the faith again.

All this means that we are confessional. We have written documents which confess our beliefs down through the years.

We are *catholic*. This word means not that we are of a particular denomination, but that we believe we are a part of one, universal Christian church around the world. Catholic means "universal." There are Roman catholics, Greek cath-

We are catholic

lics, Lutheran catholics, Presbyterian catholics. We hold to one baptism, which is valid among all legitimate families of God. Through it we are baptized into the church catholic, or universal.

In the creed that we say at our worship services, we do confess before the world that ". . . we believe in the holy catholic church, the communion of saints."

So we are catholic, confessional, sacramental, biblical, evangelical, apostolic.

And we are *ecumenical*. This seventh word is one we've heard used a lot in regard to churches in the last ten years.

Ecumenical means that we recognize most other denominations, as well as our own, as

We are ecumenical

God's legitimate daughters and sons. There are a few exceptions to this — cults such as The Way, the Unification Church, and the Mormons.

For the most part, however, we see the Holy Spirit manifesting herself in many different denominations of God's people. It is a rather beautiful thing that our needs for worship can be fulfilled in a variety of ways from the very formal to the very informal. All, nevertheless, are God's people responding to His love and grace.

We recognize each other's baptism; we recognize each other's worship experiences as legitimate; we recognize that this makes us actual brothers and sisters in God's family. So, such denominations of

Christians as Presbyterian, Methodist, United Church of Christ, Congregational, Roman Catholic, and many others, would all be treated as other brothers and sisters in Christ's family.

| God's family |

We now worship together; we now work together for justice in the community; we now refuse to try to steal each other's members, recognizing that we are one people worshipping one God. We are ecumenical.

We are also *liturgical*. Liturgical actually means "the work of the people." We look upon it as a label of the kind of worship service we offer Liturgical churches follow a "church" year. One cnurch year includes the life of Christ and

| We are liturgical |

most of his miracles and teachings. We move from season to season in our worship experience: Advent, which comes in preparation for Christmas; Christmas, which is a season of twelve days; Epiphany, which means "the dawning" when we hear the stories of the early life of Christ; Lent, which is a preparation for the crucifixion of Christ; Holy Week and Easter, which is an observance of what Christ did in Jerusalem for us and how he came out of the grave; Easter, a five-week period of time when we observe that we are the resurrection people; and Pentecost, an observance of the birthday of the Christian church and a season that continues through the summer months when we hear of the many teachings of our Lord.

We use altars and candles and vestments, and we have liturgical colors. All these are seen as symbols that aid in our worship.

We do not think any of them are essential to worship, but see them as enhancing God's presence with us as we come together in his holy house.

Our worship service is very traditional and comes from very ancient practice. We have confession; we have sung and said prayers; we have preaching from the Scripture; we hear the Bible read to us; we give our offerings in

| Our worship |

response to all God has done for us; and we gather around his table to celebrate his presence in communion. That makes us liturgical.

We are *congregational*. In this country there are three primary ways that churches govern themselves: presbyterian, episcopal, and congregational. We Lutherans are congregational in in this country. In most of the rest of the world, we are episcopal in our form of church government.

| We are congregational |

Notice that denominations take on the name of the way they are governed in this country. **Presbyterian** means that a small group of lay people and clergy are elected to have the final

| Presbyterian |

authority over a territory which includes a number of congregations.

Episcopal means that a bishop is elected or appointed over an area as the final authority for the churches that are located in that geographic unit.

Episcopal

Congregational means that the majority vote of the local congregation has the final authority of what will be the decisions of that congregation.

Congregational

So the final and highest authority for our Lutheran congregations in this country is the majority vote of the people when they come together. All this is called church "polity." It means "how we govern" ourselves.

In our own congregation there is an elected church council that makes most of the decisions for the larger congregation. The larger assembly meets only a few times a year to adopt a budget for the year, to elect council people, and also to call a pastor if that needs to be done.

You can see that we are congregational, liturgical, ecumenical, catholic, confessional, sacramental, biblical, evangelical, and apostolic.

The last word I'd like to pose for you is *historical*. This means that we are the church of the 16th century Reformation, and we see ourselves as always a reforming church in every age. It means we continually change so that we

Historical

might be the most effective witnesses for justice, peace, and the presence of God in the community in any age.

Our church was not organized by an individual in the last few years, but, rather, we trace our roots back to the Reformation and through that Reformation further back to Pentecost in the village square in Jerusalem shortly after the crucifixion and resurrection of Jesus Christ.

Our history is important to us; we see ourselves in the lineage of all the saints who have gone before us, and anticipate all those who will be baptized into the family of God after us. This makes us a historical congregation. We will need to talk more about the history of the Reformation and why it took place.

Those ten words, then, make up what we see our church to be in the world today.

PART 2

Baptism

There are two things we Christians do for God and that he does for us in our worship services. We call them "sacraments."

Sacraments are different from anything else we do and are exactly what God said we should do: baptize and commune. In the Bible we are told to do them: "Go and baptize" and "Take and eat and drink."

| Two sacraments |

Of course, we do marry, bury, confirm, and have confession, and they are important; the difference is that these things are what *people* have said we should do.

| Rites |

A sacrament is God's way of touching us in a very special way, and doing something to and for us through his church.

So now, I'd like to talk about the significance and meaning of baptism.

As Jesus was about to return to heaven, he gathered his disciples around him and told them, "Go, then, to all peoples everywhere and make them my disciples; baptize them in the name of the Father, the Son, and the Holy Spirit. . . " Matthew 28:19.

| Matthew 28:19 |

In the book of Acts there are a number of examples of how frequent and how important baptism was among the apostles and the early Christians:

At Pentecost, the very beginning of the church;
Peter at Joppa with Cornelius;
Paul and Silas in jail;
Philip and the Ethiopian eunuch.

Baptism seems to be the very heart of the Christian faith — let's learn more about it!

Martin Luther wrote in his catechism: "In baptism God forgives sin, delivers from death and the devil, and gives everlasting salvation to

| Catechism |

all who believe in what he has promised."

Jesus said to Mark, "He who believes and is baptized will be saved . . ." — Mark 16.

I. People of God live under one of two covenants; they are called "testaments," and they mean agreements or promises between two parties.

The Old Testament covenant means that, in order to be God's people and receive God's faithfulness, we would need to keep the laws he has

Covenants	
OT	**NT**
Exodus 24:1-8	
10 rules	
Moses	
Old testament	
Circumcision	

given us and be circumcised as a part of his people. The old covenant or old testament is recorded in the first part of the Bible. It tells us how it went with the people who tried to live with this relationship to God. It was started by Moses when he brought the people out of Egypt and through the wilderness. He went up on Mount Sinai and struck this covenant with God: that they should keep these ten rules and that God would remain faithful and care for them.

The new testament is a whole different thing. It depends on God's being grace-full. Baptism is the seal of the new covenant relationship to God, just like circumcision is for the old covenant. the New Testament portion of the Bible, which is in the back of the book, is the record of this agreement. It was started

New covenant	
OT	**NT**
Exodus 24:1-8	Mark 16:16
10 rules	God's grace
Moses	New testament
Old testament	Jesus and Christ
Circumcision	Baptism

and consummated by Jesus, the Christ, who was born in Bethlehem and who died in Jerusalem on a cross and came out of the grave there

The Jews still live under the "old deal," or old covenant. We Christians live under the "new deal," or new covenant. Jews circumcise and we baptize.

Our deal depends on a God who loves us so much that he forgives us because of what Christ did for us on the cross.

II. Baptism is our new birth. First we are born into the world from conception by two human parents. That's where we get our family name, and is when we become a part of — an addition to — the human race.

New birth

At baptism we are reborn (born again) into a new family with a heavenly father. So then we get our Christian name. It's very much like an adoption. God adopts us from our worldly family into his heavenly family and becomes our father.

St. Paul uses the analogy of being baptized with Christ into his death, so that we can be raised to a new life just as he did. Paul claims that we can be so joined to Christ that we can go through our death and resurrection to eternal

> St. Paul

life, just as Jesus did when he died on the cross and came out of the grave that first Easter.

So we ought not hesitate to say we are, indeed, "saved." We are "born again," we are born anew. We have received the Spirit of God, and it all has happened at our baptism.

We often say we are baptized because of original sin. That term is simply the name of our condition. It means that we are humans. Because of our being human, we cannot make it on our own. Our natural inclination is to rebel against God because of our humanness.

> Original sin

So we need to be reborn into God's family where we are forgiven and rescued and accepted into his security.

Notice that we do *not* say original sin means that one man and one woman rebelled against God 4,000 years ago, and that God's still getting even for their eating an apple they weren't supposed to eat. Instead, we believe that the story says, "This is the way it is with human beings."

We have chosen, and continue to choose, to rebel against God. Because of our humanity, we need a divinity when we are reborn into his family by baptism.

Let's illustrate it this way: my wife is a sinner and I am a sinner, so each child we conceive and bring into the world will be a sinner. My wife is a Schmalenberger and I am a Schmalenberger, so each child we conceive and bring into the world will be a Schmalenberger. It's a good analogy.

III. Let's talk about how we baptize, and especially why we baptize infants. We baptize a baby because it is a gift that we give that child. It is a gift that the child need not understand or deserve. Just as parents adopt a tiny baby without asking the baby if he wants it, or just as giv-

> The mode of
> baptism

ing a Christmas gift to a tiny infant long before she understands what Christmas is or what grandparents are or anything like that, so, too, God adopts and gives a gift at the baptismal service.

Whole families were sometimes baptized in the early church. This is an example that's worth looking at. At Pentecost, that very first day of the Christian church, all ages and conditions of people, including infants, were baptized. In the home of Cornelius, the first gentile to be baptized,

St. Peter baptized him and all his kin. Let's remember, too, that Jesus said, "Let the children come unto me and do not stop them." — Luke 18:16.

Let's not forget the Rite of Confirmation. We now call it Affirmation of Baptism. This is the second part of an infant baptism. When the child grows up and takes on the responsibilities of an adult, he comes to the church and studies the

Confirmation

Christian faith with the pastor, and eventually comes before God's altar and affirms that which was given to him when he was an infant. Parents and godparents stand alongside, rejoicing that this gift which was given to an infant has now been affirmed by that infant as he matured in years.

The promises at Affirmation of Baptism is to be responsible for the great gift that was given a long time ago. So we see that affirmation of baptism, or confirmation, becomes the second part of an infant baptism. It completes the receiving of the gift.

IV. Let's look at how to baptize. You know, the Scripture never tells us how to do the baptizing. Some feel that it must be done by immersion or dunking.

The Greek New Testament word, "baptizo," is claimed by some to mean "to dunk." That probably is true. Actually, "baptizo" means "to wash." It is used that way in many of the other writings that were written at the same time as the New Testament. You can wash in many ways. You can shower, dunk in, sprinkle, or wipe on the towel.

On Pentecost baptism probably was not done by immersion. There were just too many people and too little water and not enough time in that village square in Jerusalem. Probably Peter, James, and John worked some other method of getting the water on the people.

Immersion

Jesus didn't think it important enough to tell us how to do it. We Lutheran Christians simply accept any method by which water and God's word are used.

In the Scripture, one of our good examples of baptism by other than immersion would be the time when Paul and Silas were in prison and baptized the jailer right there in the jail cell.

Because this wasn't an issue for Christians in the early church, it isn't for us Christians, either. We'll accept any way that water and the word are used.

By the way, we Lutheran Christians never rebaptize. We recognize any other denomination's baptism as valid and never redo it.

Re-baptism

Once water and the word are used, it's valid. It's legitimate. We do not try to redo some other religious group's act, but accept a person as a legitimate brother or sister in the Christian faith.

V. We believe baptism is the way into the church, the Body of Christ, and into heaven itself.

> Entrance

The reason for the baptismal font's often being located at the front door of a church is that it visually demonstrates the fact that this is the way into the church and the kingdom.

Baptism is the most important thing we do or have done in our entire life on earth.

The water is symbolic of washing: washing away our sins and making us clean with a new life. Notice this new life — from then on we are different people; we are a new family, even with a new name. We now have brothers and sisters whom we have joined by God's adoption called baptism.

> Washing

Notice, too, we believe the Holy Spirit is given at Baptism. It is not just a forgiving sacrament, not just a new start in life with a new family, but a spirit that now is with us and in us and equips us to face whatever comes in this earthly life.

> Holy Spirit

We believe that baptism is a gift given forever, right on into eternal life. The promise is that we'll never be separated from our God.

Church and worship become the place and time, where and when we give thanks to our heavenly father for his adoption. Wherever and whenever the family gets together, we join them in a great thanksgiving meal, thankful that we have been adopted into such a sisterhood and brotherhood.

The communion is the family-home table, the time that the family celebrates and fellowships together with the father of the family present with them.

VI. The Apostles' Creed, which we use in our worship service, is actually three answers to three questions that are asked at our baptism. So we repeat over and over every time we get together around his table, or gather in his living room, those promises which were made for us at our baptism and which we affirmed at our confirmation:

> Apostles' Creed

"Do you believe in God?"
"Do you believe in Jesus Christ?"
"Do you believe in the Holy Spirit and the Christian church?"

So we stand and say that creed each time we come together for worship, to confess that it is the one thing we hold in common. It is our unity here as a family of God. We may, and probably do, differ on how the baptized ought to live and treat each other. But on this faith, expressed in this creed, is our unity: to believe in God, to believe in Jesus Christ, to believe in the Holy Spirit.

It's our initiation and our baptism into the family of God.

I was baptized April 15, 1934, in St. Paul's Lutheran Church in Greenville, Ohio. My father and mother were there, making the same promises I made for my children. My godparents were there — Aunt Tangie and Uncle Monty. They still keep close and watch after me.

And I joined that day, in April of 1934, the same God's family as my Grandpa Jacob Frederick Schmalenberger, and before him, his father, Nicolaus, in the little town of Schmalenberg, Germany. All the way back to the Reformation at a similar baptismal font in that little German Protestant congregation, we joined the faith. That's the kind of tradition and heritage baptism becomes.

Jesus started it all — by having his cousin, John the Baptist, baptize him in the Jordan as an example of belonging and forgiveness of sins. When he went to the cross, he gave baptism much more significance by what he did on that cross.

We celebrate and observe it yet today.

". . . after all the people had been baptized, Jesus also was baptized, and while he was praying, heaven was opened . . ." (Luke 3:21 TEV)

PART 3

Holy Communion

We have mentioned the two sacraments of the Protestant church which are called Baptism and Holy Communion. We said that we do have all the other acts of the church like burial of the dead, marriage, confession, and ordination, and that we call them "rites."

Rites

At the time of the Reformation in the 16th century when the Protestant church was born, the church mothers and fathers set up three tests of what a sacrament would be in the reformed church:

"Are we told to do it in the Scripture?"
"If we do it, are we promised anything as a
    a result in the Scripture?"
"Is there an earthly element?"

Test for a sacrament

When we look at communion, we find that Jesus does tell the disciples to drink and eat in this fashion, that he does promise the forgiveness of sins and his presence with us when we do, and that there are earthly elements of bread and wine. For this reason, communion is our second sacrament after baptism.

Let's take just a moment to review what we said about baptism: we said that we are adopted into God's family through this sacrament; that it is when Christians are reborn or born anew as saved people; that we are first born into the

Baptism

human race, and then we are reborn into God's family through baptism. We also said the Rite of Confirmation is the second part of infant baptism when we become adult members of the Body of Christ.

Now let's look at the background of Holy Communion. The earliest account in the Bible that we have about communion is Paul's writing in 1 Corinthians 11. It is recorded in the 23rd through the 25th verses.

1 Corinthians 11

In the Gospels in the Bible we also learn of the upper room observance of communion on what has come to be called "Maundy

Thursday," the Thursday before Good Friday when Jesus was crucified. We learn in those Gospels that Jesus and his disciples gathered in the spare room of Mary, the mother of John

| Maundy Thursday |

Mark (who wrote the Gospel of Mark), and there they prepared to celebrate the Passover.

In the Jewish celebration of Passover, unleavened bread and wine are shared. The Passover is the Jewish observance of Moses' leading them out of their slavery in Egypt toward the "promised land." Since the disciples and

| Passover |

Jesus were Jews, they had gathered that night for this observance. Our Lord gave a whole new meaning to eating that bread and drinking that wine. He assured those disciples that if they would share the bread in a certain fashion and drink the wine in a certain manner, he would be with them like no other time in their lives. It became an observance of the people of the new covenant; that is, the baptized, celebrating together the fact that they were a part of God's adopted family.

So Jesus took this old testament people's observance and made it a new testament celebration of how things are between us, who are the baptized, and our loving father

He promised he would be with us, and we would actually experience his presence if we would take the bread and drink the wine in a similar fashion. For this reason, baptized Christians have gathered together frequently ever

| His presence |

since as a part of their worship experience and have eaten bread and drunk wine, celebrating their forgiveness and enjoying the fellowship of the rest of the forgiven people of God. It has become very similar to the way we gather around our mother's or father's table for a Thanksgiving meal on that special holiday.

There are three different ideas about what happens when we take communion.

Communion Traditions		
Orthodox	Lutheran	Reformed
Br̶e̶a̶d = Body W̶i̶n̶e̶ = Blood	Bread = Body Wine = Blood	Bread = B̶o̶d̶y̶ Grape juice = Bl̶o̶o̶d̶
Transubstantiation	Real Presence	Memorial

The orthodox Christians, those who are part of the Roman Catholic, Russian, and Greek Orthodox churches in our country, call their belief about communion "transubstantiation." They believe that only an ordained priest has the power to hold up the bread and wine at a special time in the mass and work a miracle of changing that bread and wine into the actual body and blood of Christ. They call this the "Sacrifice of the Mass." You will often hear a bell ring and sometimes incense will be used at the moment when the orthodox Christian is confident that bread bread and wine disappear and the real body and blood of Christ appear. This is the reason these

| Orthodox tradition |

Christians, so very reverent and respectful, are extremely careful with that bread and wine, the way they receive it, and care for any that is left over.

The reformed churches of our country call their belief about communion "memorial." They concentrate on the portion of Scripture that says, ". . . do this in memory of me." So when they

| Reformed tradition |

take that bread and grape juice into their mouths, they believe it remains bread and grape juice, and that it is simply a time when they are especially reminded of what God has done for them on the cross and out of the grave. It becomes a beautiful time of remembering. Because they do not believe it is the actual body and blood of Christ, they are not quite as careful about how the whole sacrament is carried out. Often lay people will take it out into the homes of shut-ins and absent members and so forth. It usually is celebrated much less frequently than those Christians who are of orthodox tradtion.

We Lutheran Christians call our idea about communion "the real presence." We believe the bread and wine actually stay bread and wine. However, we are confident Christ is really present in that bread and wine. That is, we are sure that when we take the bread and wine into

| Lutheran tradition Real presence |

our bodies, we are actually allowing that bread and wine to carry Christ's presence into our body and into our fellowship of communion. We do believe everything the reformed tradition believes when they talk about memorial. We believe a part of our communion service is to remember all that God has done tor us. We also believe, like those of the orthodox tradition, that he is present there at the sacrament. We put these two ideas together and come up with that which we hold as our common belief about communion.

Let's take a little time to talk about how we receive this sacrament. It's probably true that Jesus broke off a piece of a common loaf and passed the loaf around for each one to take a piece and eat. He probably drank from a com-

| Common cup |

mon cup and passed that around and asked the disciples also to drink from it. This has been the earliest fashion of administering communion. In a number of countries of the world, other than the United States, it is still the most common practice — everyone drinks from one chalice and eats from one loaf. Sometimes we offer communion by "common cup."

when everyone drinks out of the same cup and eats a piece from a common loaf.

Here in this country, about fifty or seventy years ago, when we became very conscious of germs, many Lutheran Christians began using the individual glasses with little wafers to represent the bread. In many Lutheran congregations

Individual portions

we can still take communion that way by coming forward and kneeling at the communion rail, and each eating one of the wafers and drinking from one of the little individual cups.

Communion is also given in the Lutheran church by a method called "intinction." We set up a station such as the balcony, and there the pastor dips the wafer in the wine and places it on the people's tongues. This is often done for the sick.

Intinction

We never want to get upset or excited about the method of receiving the bread and wine, because this probably wasn't important to our Lord or he would have given us direct instructions on how to do it. The important thing is that he is with us and we are sharing in a common celebration of that presence.

Each time we have communion at our church we also take the bread and wine from the altar out to our shut-ins and hospital patients, so they can join with the rest of the family in this fellowship.

Private communion

We do pay attention to 1 Corinthians 11, where Paul advises us that we must always ". . . examine ourself first, and then eat the bread and drink from the cup." — 1 Corinthians 11:28. For this reason, we usually have confession before we take communion in order to prepare ourselves to take it.

1 Corinthians 11

Confession

Please notice that we Christians do not see communion as "last rites." We give it only to people who understand what they are doing when they take it. We do not try to get it down a person's throat who is about to die in the emergency room at the hospital or one who is unconscious. It is more a celebration of the fact that we are the baptized, alive, and together at this time and that Christ is with us.

Until about 15 years ago, Lutheran Christians would ask their young people to take catechism and be confirmed about eighth grade level before they received the sacrament of communion. All that has changed now. Worldwide, we Lutheran Christians call our fifth graders together with their parents and

First communion

give them instruction into what the significance of communion is for them. Then we admit them to their first communion, and from then on they receive it with the rest of the congregation. This change was made primarily to accommodate Lutherans in countries behind the Iron Curtain where they may never be able to be confirmed, but ought not be deprived of the two sacraments. It also better reflects what we believe about communion: that it is a gift from God, and we need not earn it by having confirmation first.

The thing I most love to do in the Christian ministry is to prepare young people and their parents for the children's first communion, and then to admit them to the Table. It is one of the glorious experiences of our maturing in our baptism.

Another policy of our Lutheran Church in America is that we have "open communion." This means we offer communion to all people who are baptized, fifth grade and above, and

| Open communion |

who are willing to come forward for the sacrament. We do not limit it just to our own congregation or to our own denomination. We see communion as one of the ways Christians of various disciplines, denominations, and beliefs, can join together as one body and family in Christ.

There are a number of congregations who have what is called "closed communion." This means they give the sacrament only to their own membership. If you are an outsider or visitor, it

| Closed communion |

will be necessary for you to announce that fact and be examined by the pastor as to your beliefs about communion before you can be admitted to it.

Another policy of our church and the Lutheran Church in America is that only ordained pastors may be celebrants, who must preside any time communion is offered. Because of the

| Celebrant |

number of abuses of the sacrament in the early church, we have found it a good safeguard, to make sure communion is celebrated with respect and dignity, to ask that only the ordained administer it.

It's a beautiful way that God has given us to celebrate what he has done for us on the cross and in coming out of the grave. It's not something we deserve, or even earn, in coming forward to receive it. It is simply a gift of fellowship

| Eucharist |

with the Almighty and with all of his family. The first name for communion in the Greek language was "eucharist." That means "the thanksgiving." So we come together to give thanks. It is a time of quiet and reverence, celebration and thanksgiving — for how God is and for the fact that he has chosen to be with us.

PART 4

The Scriptures

As we looked at the beliefs and sacraments of the Christian church, we found that there have been two different agreements with God over the years. The one is called the old testament and the other the new testament.

Covenants	
OT	**NT**
Laws	Grace
Moses	Christ
Circumcision	Baptism

Our Bible is made up of sixty-six books, which are also divided between Old Testament and New Testament.

The first thirty-nine books have to do with the deal made with God through Moses when the people were being led out of Egypt toward the Promised Land. You recall, that deal was that if the people would keep the rules then God would remain faithful to them. So we have thirty-nine books that describe how It went with the people's trying to keep that particular agreement.

> Old Testament

The twenty-seven books of the New Testament are about a different agreement and relationship with God. They describe the new covenant and how it went with those trying to keep It. You recall that the new covenant was belief in Jesus Christ, his death on the cross, and resurrection from the grave that first Easter. We are baptized; and God will forgive, watch over, save, and be with us here. I'd like to look at that collection of twenty-seven books called the New Testament and see just how they came to us.

> New Testament

It's probably true that the earliest writings about the new covenant, certainly before the four Gospels in the New Testament Bible, are the writings of St. Paul. Paul would start a little congregation; after it was going well he would move on to another town. His people would continually write to him, and he would in turn write to them to keep the little church going after he left. We have a collection of those letters in the New Testament Bible.

> Paul's letters

They were written before the gospels that tell of the life and ministry of Jesus.

The earliest gospel was the one we call Mark. It probably was written somewhere around 45-55 A.D. It is a very crude book with poor grammar, poor spelling, and was only about the *life* of Christ. It did not try to cover what Jesus taught or have much theology about him at all. It contains simple facts of the life of Jesus.

Evidently when some of the eyewitnesses began to die, others thought it necessary to write down this story to pass on to future generations. John Mark had a mother by the name of Mary who owned a home on Mount Zion where the Upper Room was located. Not only had he been an eyewitness to the Lord's Supper in that room, but he lived in that house which was the gathering place for the disciples when they were in the Jerusalem area.

In addition, Mark later accompanied Paul, who heard Peter's preaching, on his first missionary journey. This is the primary source of his gospel story.

The next document that came into existence we call the "Quelle." This was probably written by the disciple Matthew, who was a tax collector, well-educated, and could use a pen. He wrote down what Jesus taught. It was probably called "the teachings of Jesus," but that particular document has been lost. Although it is referred to in the Scripture, we do not have it as a single individual writing.

The next book that we have, according to chronology, would be the Gospel of Matthew. Someone (we don't know who) took John Mark's "life of Jesus" and put it together with Matthew's "teaching of Jesus," calling it "The Gospel of Matthew."

If you know the Greek language, you can go through the Gospel of Matthew, as we have it today, and find almost every word of Mark's gospel. You can also find the great majority of the lost document, which was called "the teachings of Jesus.

Not only that, but Matthew's gospel is written from the point of view of seeing the pro-

New Testament
timeline

Mark

Quelle

Matthew

phecy of the Old Testament fulfilled. It is often called "the church's gospel" or the "teaching gospel" because it gives such a complete, well-rounded story of Jesus' life, ministry, and teachings. The story of the birth of Jesus in Matthew's gospel is written from the male perspective and traces Jesus' lineage through his father, Joseph.

The next gospel that came along, according to time order, was the Gospel of Luke. You may recall that Luke was a medical doctor. Luke went along with St. Paul to care for his medical needs and to serve as a missionary with him. His gospel story is written from the perspective of a medical person and includes many of the healing miracles told only in that book. In addition, Luke writes very much from the perspective of women, and includes many of the stories about women and Jesus that are only found in his gospel. He writes the birth narrative of Jesus from the perspective of Mary, rather than Joseph.

Luke actually wrote a two-volume book. The second volume is called the Acts of the Apostles. Here Luke tells about the early church after that first Pentecost and how the disciples, apostles, and early Christians got along in the world. He also relates a lot about his partner in mission, St. Paul.

The Gospel of Luke and the Book of Acts are both written to a person by the name of Theophilos, which means they are a two-part letter describing the life of Christ and the life of the early church. Some theorize that Theophilos was a high Roman official and that Luke was writing to him to convince him of the faith. Others think this is just a pseudonym for "a lover of God."

We also have another writer, John, who wrote a two-volume work. John wrote his Gospel of John, the latest of the gospels, and also the book of Revelation.

The Gospel of John is not a story of the life of Jesus, but more of a theology about Jesus. He omits the birth story and begins right with the baptism of Jesus, by John the Baptist, in the Jordan. To John, the reason Jesus was here on earth is much more important than just how or where events happened. John may have been one of the disciples, a young boy during the life

Teaching Gospel

Luke

Acts

Theophilos

John

of Jesus; and, if so, he was the only disciple to die a natural death. He wrote the Gospel of John and the book of Revelation at a very old age.

The book of Revelation, the last book in our Bible, was written out on the Island of Patmos where John was in exile from his seven-church parish.

Revelation is a very dangerous book to read, unless one has help with it all the way through. It is written in apocalyptic language, in a code, and some of the code has never been figured out. John had to write this way because, at the time he was writing, Christians were being persecuted by and forced to worship the Emperor. He wrote in code so, if one were caught with this writing, it would not make sense to the inquisitor.

The whole book of Revelation is actually a recording of John's vision of the risen Christ's being with him and speaking to him. It also contains seven letters to his former seven-church parish on the mainland.

There are only a couple books in the Bible which are apocalyptic: the book of Revelation in the New Testament and the book of Daniel in the Old Testament. Apocalyptic writing was used when the people were being persecuted; and the chosen of God could see no other way for them to win, but that God would intervene and get even with their enemies in due time. This was small comfort to those who were being defeated.

Most of the book of Revelation refers to what would happen if, indeed, the people were forced to Emperor worship against the will of God. Much of what was said in this book had already happened in the fall of Jerusalem.

It is a serious mistake to take such writings as Hal Lindsey's book, *The Late, Great Planet Earth*, then read into the Book of Revelation future guesses as to what will happen in our day. That is a terrible misuse of the Scripture. The book of Revelation can be an inspiration to read, but should not be read alone or without good biblical helps, so that we understand what God is trying to say to us through it.

Well, we now have the four Gospels of the New Testament that tell the story and the teachings of Jesus, and we also have the Acts of the Apostles that tells the story of the early church. The book of Revelation gives to us a rather coded picture of the future.

Revelation

Apocalyptic

Most of the rest of the New Testament was written by St. Paul. These books are letters that he wrote back to former congregations, instructing them how to live as Christians and correcting them on their practices of worship, Christian ethics, and theology. These are such books as Corinthians, Galatians, Ephesians, Philippians, and Thessalonians. Then we have some personal notes Paul wrote to people who needed to be instructed in the faith, such as I and II Timothy, Titus, and Philemon. The Book of Hebrews may have been written by Paul, but some are leaning towards the possibility that it may have been written by Priscilla or one of the educated women of the early church, instructing Sunday School teachers about their beliefs. It's a beautiful book.

St. Paul's letters

St. Paul was a Jewish rabbi who converted to the Christian faith on the Damascus Road and then became our greatest missionary. He is the one mainly responsible for taking the Christian faith to the world outside Palestine, especially to the Gentiles. St. Paul probably is one of the most intelligent men ever to live on the face of the earth.

Gentiles

After several hundred years, the church of Jesus Christ finally decided that the "Canon" of the New Testament would be complete. This means that no more could be added to it, and twenty-seven books would be the final and accepted books of the New Testament.

Canon

So much for the New Testament. Let's now turn our attention to the Old Testament books.

The first writings, which are what we call the Books of Moses, or the Pentateuch, came about a thousand years before Christ. One thing we have to understand about these first books of the Old Testament is that they were written and rewritten, and added to and subtracted from, many, many times. This means that they were written by men of faith, but it does not mean every word we find printed in a particular version will agree with all the rest of the Bible.

Old Testament

It looks as if it all began this way: Around 950 B.C. a group of people in the Northern Kingdom wrote the first few books of the Bible to answer a number of questions like these:

"Where did I come from?"
"Who created me?"
"Why am I afraid of snakes and bats?"

The people who wrote this first document believed that God's name was "Jaweh" or "Yahweh." They wrote down the stories, myths, the legends of their day, and that folk wisdom which had been handed down from one generation to another called "the Oral Tradition."

About 100 years later, people from the Southern Kingdom rewrote the whole document, and they named God "Elohim." They inserted their folk wisdom, heroes, and their version of many of the early creation stories. This is why you can find a couple different accounts of creation, Noah and the ark, Abraham and his son Isaac, and many other stories.

The Josiah Reform came about 636 B.C., when one Temple was established in Jerusalem. King Josiah had a book called "Deuteronomy" written to include the rules of the Jewish faith. When this book was proclaimed as official during Josiah's reign, the entire Books of Moses were rewritten, adding the Deuteronomy rules.

About 400 B.C. the priestly code was added. This code came after the institution of priests had been established in the church, and rewriting was done again, adding the role of the priest in each of the stories. By now one can see that the books, called the Bible, have been rewritten many times with lots of additions in each instance. All together these are called the Pentateuch, or the first five, and most important, books of our Old Testament.

Someone wanted to add the hymnbook of the Temple, so the Book of Psalms was included.

Others thought the excellent wisdom literature of the day and poetry should be added, so we have the Book of Proverbs and Ecclesiastes. Books like Esther were added in order to legitimize the holiday of Purim, when the Jew had the priviledge of cursing his enemies before the altar in the Temple. Daniel is an apocalyptic book, much like the Book of Revelation.

The great majority of the rest of the Old Testament is sermons and prophecies by the Old Testament prophets. These were the holy men of their day who insisted that, if the people continued on their present course, certain things would happen in the future. Those who prophe-

Jaweh

Elohim

Josiah Reform

Priestly code

Pentateuch

Psalms

Proverbs
Ecclesiastes
Esther
Daniel

Prophets

sied correctly, proven in time, got their names and works in the Bible.

You can see that all this added together makes up our thirty-nine Old Testament books. We believe that inspired people wrote and rewrote these documents, and that God is speaking to us through them. We do not see them as infallible or without error.

> Infallibility

The Bible is, indeed, the norm for our life and the very heart and center of our faith. We do not worship the book itself; but, rather, worship the Christ that it reveals.

> Norm for life

It has been fun explaining to you the origin of our Holy Scripture. I hope you have been motivated to dig into your Bible and to read, expecting God to speak in a very beautiful way to your life.

PART 5

The Reformation

You don't have to look very carefully to notice that Christians are divided up into many different denominations, families, and church buildings in any community. Now we are going to look at the reason for those divisions.

> Denominations

It all began with what is called the "Reformation" in the 16th century. It was the year 1517,

> Reformation

October 31, and a Roman Catholic Augustinian friar by the name of Martin Luther posted 95 theses on the castle church door in Wittenberg, Germany. The Reformation had begun.

Long before on November 10, 1483, in the little town of Eisleben, Germany, a recently-married couple stopped on their journey to the town of Mansfeld, Germany, where the young husband was going to seek work in the copper mines. Margarethe Luder had her baby in Eisleben on November 10. She and her husband Hans, took him to St. Ann's Church several blocks away

> Luther's birth

> Baptism

the next day, St. Martin's Day, and named him Martin after the saint of his baptism.

Martin grew up wanting to be a lawyer, and attended the University of Erfurt to prepare for that profession. One night on the way home to his parents' he was nearly struck by lightning and was very frightened. He vowed that if St. Ann would save him he would become a monk. She did save him, and he did become a monk!

Luther attended the Cloister of the Augustinian Friars in Erfurt, and was ordained into the priesthood. He had a terrible struggle with guilt and forgiveness.

> Ordination

His superior thought it would be good for him to teach at a new little university called Wittenberg, which had been started by Elector Frederick the Wise. It was at this university that Luther took the action which caused the split from the Roman Catholic Church.

After studying the Scriptures, he had three big differences of opinion with the organized church of the day:

1. The Roman Catholic Church claimed the priesthood was a very special order of human beings. Luther was quite confident the church should be made up of the priesthood of all people.

Priesthood of all believers

2. The Roman Catholic Church claimed that only the church had the right to interpret Scripture and to have final authority over people's lives. Luther believed, from reading the Scripture, that the final authority for all people was the Bible, not the church.

Scripture alone

3. The Roman Catholic Church claimed that salvation was through a rather intricate scheme of good works and God's grace. Luther read in the Scriptures that we are saved by "grace alone" through faith.

Grace alone

Notice that these were the problems in the 16th century. Lutherans and Roman Catholics have only recently come very close to agreement on these differences. A growing rapport has developed, and a commission has just released the following statement: "We can and do confess together that our hope for salvation rests entirely on God's merciful action in Christ." A 21,000-word joint statement was issued October 1, 1983, to tell of our similarities and agreements.

New day

Because the printing press was a rather new invention at that time and printers were looking for something to print, what Luther had written and posted on the Wittenberg church door was picked up and spread throughout the country.

Printing press

Politically, it was just the right time. German nationalism was on the rise, and the Germans simply did not want to be subjected to a church hierarchy that had its headquarters in Rome. In addition, they certainly did not want their church offerings to go to Italy.

Nationalism

Luther continued as a professor at Wittenberg University and as a parish priest at the city church in the little Wittenberg town all his life. He is often called the "Father of the German Language" because he translated the Old and New Testaments from their original Greek and Hebrew while he was in hiding at the Wartburg Castle during the Reformation turmoil.

Parish priest

Luther is also thought of as the one who started the institution of the church parsonage

Married clergy

and clergy families. He married a former nun, Katharina von Bora, and the two of them had five children.

In addition, Luther made great contributions to hymn singing and music in worship. He was a musician in his own right and wrote many hymns. For worship he simply took the German Low Mass and translated it into the language of

> Singing

the people. This was one of his great strengths: he believed Christians should always worship in their own native language rather than in Latin.

Luther died in the same town in which he was born — Eisleben, Germany. He had gone to that little town to settle a dispute between two dukes and to preach at the parish church. While there he contracted pneumonia and died. One can still

> Luther's death

see the house and bed where he passed from this life to life eternal. It was in the shadow of the St. Ann's Church where he had been baptized many years before.

The Reformation spread throughout Europe, especially to Germany and the Scandinavian countries. When the Germans and Scandinavians immigrated to the United States, they brought their Lutheran Christianity with them, and thus

> Spread of Reformation

the Lutheran church was spread throughout our country as well.

It ought to be said here that the primary beliefs of our Reformation church, right up to the present, are that Scripture is our final authority, each one is a priest in God's sight, and that we are saved by grace alone rather than by any effort on our part.

> Primary beliefs

We Lutherans do have what is called the Book of Concord, which has in it a number of documents that state what we believe. The three

> Book of Concord

ecumenical creeds are of extreme importance in our belief system. Of course, the Bible is our central authority.

Included in the Book of Concord is the Augsburg Confession. This document was signed by the princes of the various provinces of Germany in Augsburg in 1530. The Roman Catholics and Lutherans had come together to see if they could make peace in the midst of the Reformation so that they could put up a united front against the Turks who were militarily at their door. We have then this confession which states what Lutherans and Roman Catholics hold in common and on what things they differ. It's still our basic statement of faith, outside the Scripture and the creeds.

After the Lutheran Church had come into being, Luther was appalled at the lack of spiritual growth and knowledge of those in the priesthood and in the pew. He wrote a Small Catechism which deals primarily with the sacraments, the Lord's Prayer, the Ten Commandments, and the

> Catechism

creeds. This catechism has been used ever since in preparing youth and adults for the rite of Affirmation of Baptism and for baptism into adult membership in a Lutheran congregation.

Preaching was very important to Martin Luther and the new reformed Lutheran church. You will see a strong emphasis on proclamation of the Good News from the Scripture at each worship service where Lutherans attend. Lutheran clergy are highly-trained professionals with four years of college after high school, three years of seminary after college, and a year of Internship before ordination into the ministry. Often they pursue and achieve a doctoral level of ministry in the years that follow.

> Preaching

Because the Scripture is so important to Lutherans, most Lutheran clergy must have a knowledge of the original languages of the Bible, the Hebrew and the Greek. In addition, many learn the German language in order to read and understand Martin Luther.

> Language

The system by which Lutherans govern themselves in the United States is called "congregational." This means each Lutheran congregation is the final authority for its decisions. Bishops and presidents are, indeed, over synods and conventions, but a majority vote of the congregation holds final authority for what the congregation does or does not do.

> Congregational

In Europe and other countries of the world, for the most part, Lutherans administer their church business through bishops, much like the Episcopal Church in this country. In this kind of system the bishop who is elected by an assembly of congregational representatives has final authority over the congregation.

> Episcopal

I appreciate having the opportunity to tell about us Lutherans, the Reformation, and how our newly reformed church was given birth in the 16th century. It ought to be said that we are now very good friends with Roman Catholics and other Orthodox Christians and consider each other legitimate brothers and sisters in the Body of Christ.

> Brothers and Sisters

Because of the 500th anniversary of Martin Luther's birth in 1983, it is especially appropriate that we devote this section to him and to his contribution to the Christian church in the world.

PART 6

The Creeds

Shortly after Pentecost, the birthday of the church, the first statement of what the people, who were baptized into Christianity in the square in Jerusalem, believed was simply "Jesus is Lord." What they said was in opposition to the require- ments of Emperor worship when the Roman government tried to make every citizen go into the Temple to offer some sacrifice and confess, "Caesar is Lord." The first Christian creed was "Jesus is Lord." It is still the creed of the World Council of Churches.

> Jesus is Lord

Since those very early primitive years of Christianity, three main ecumenical creeds have developed as statements of what Christians hold to as correct concerning God. These three are called the Athanasian Creed, the Nicene Creed, and the Apostles' Creed.

> Ecumenical creeds

The Athanasian Creed was written about the 4th century and was a very lengthy statement that was written to counteract some heresies that were being promoted among Christians. We use it today only as a study document in our seminaries, and occasionally it is sung by a choir at a worship service.

> Athanasian

The Nicene Creed was adopted by the church at the Council of Nicea in 364 A.D. A man by the name of Arius was teaching a wrong belief about God's creating Jesus and Jesus' creating the Holy Spirit. To counteract that wrong teach- ing, the church adopted the Nicene Creed. It says in many different ways, often in a very repetive fashion, that we Christians hold that there are not three Gods, one created by the other, but one God who has appeared in at least three different ways at various times in history. There was a time when this God was working as Creator and we can observe the results of that. There was a time when this God put on human flesh and appeared as a man in the Middle East and we can read Scripture accounts of that.

> Nicene

There is a time now when we can witness his presence in his Spirit with us and we know that he is here. All three are the same God. The Nicene Creed tells us that.

It would be very much like the fact that sometimes I am a pastor, sometimes a father, sometimes a brother, and quite often a husband. I'm still the same person, but I fill different roles at different times in my life. So it has been with God. So the reason for the writing of the Nicene Creed was to make that clear.

We want to take most of our time to look at the Apostles' Creed. We use it at almost every worship service. It is simply three answers to three questions given when a person is baptized. It is called "apostolic" because it is a statement of what those believed who saw Jesus face-to-face and lived when he lived on earth.

| Apostles' |

When persons would come forward to be baptized into Christianity in the very early Church, they were asked three questions:

| 3 questions |

"Do you believe in God?"
"Do you believe in Christ?"
"Do you believe in the Holy Spirit and the Christian Church?"

If they stated that they believed in these three things, the converts were then baptized in the name of God the Father, God the Son who was Jesus Christ, and God the Holy Spirit.

We call these three paragraphs "articles" of the creed. Sometimes they are named the "Article of Creation," the "Article of Redemption," and the "Article of Sanctification." Sometimes they are simply referred to as what we believe about the Father, the Son, and the Holy Spirit.

| Articles |

We are going to look at each of these in some detail because they are the very linchpin of our faith. The only way we can come into Christianity is through baptism, and the only way we can do that is to confess that we believe what is stated in these articles of the Apostles' Creed.

Let's look at the first article, which says, "I believe in God, the Father Almighty, creator of heaven and earth."

| First Article |

We are really saying in this part of the creed that we believe that before there was anything else there was God. We believe that God is the genesis of all there is. It was God who called everything into being. The important sentence in the Old Testament for this belief is the very first part of the first sentence of the book of Genesis where it simply says, "In the beginning God . . ."

Let it be said here that we do not believe the Bible is a science textbook. The book of Genesis is an account of people of faith writing down the latest creation information they had in their day,

| Science and creation |

to say that they believed it was God who did it. We still are not sure how. The *how* is not as important as the *who*. These rather simple people wanted to convince us that God was the creator, so they took the information they had and told it, saying it was God who did it all. If I wanted to do the same thing today, I'd take the latest information I had, such as the "Big Bang" theory, and have God as the originator of it all. I'd probably begin by saying, "In the beginning God caused a piece of the sun to spin off into the atmosphere and to cool . . ."

You see, we have no fight with scientific investigation. On the contrary, we encourage science to continue to learn, experiment, and investigate to find out just how God does things. Whenever a new discovery comes into light, we don't fight it and say it threatens our faith; but instead we congratulate the scientist and rejoice that we have learned more about the way God works.

We are not "creationists." It is not important to us that the six-day creation story be held as true. We see it simply as the latest information of that time and not very important to our faith. Before anything else there was God, and that is what we still hold as true.

| Creationists |

The second article is called the "Article of Redemption." It tells what we believe about the person of Jesus Christ and what he came to do and accomplish. "I believe in Jesus Christ, his only Son, our Lord. He was conceived by the power of the Holy Spirit and born of the virgin Mary. He suffered under Pontius Pilate, was crucified, died, and was buried. He descended into hell. On the third day he rose again. He ascended into heaven, and is seated at the right hand of the Father, He will come again to judge the living and the dead."

| Second article |

These words state for us our belief that Jesus actually was God who put on human flesh to experience humanity like we know it. We believe it was actually a historical time, and he was a person who was born in Bethlehem, grew up in Nazareth, and ministered around Galilee. He was crucified on the cross in Jerusalem and came out of the grave there.

We don't make a big deal about the fact of the virgin birth. We emphasize much more the fact of the Incarnation. The miracle of Christmas is that God decided to become a human being and to limit himself on purpose so he could, indeed, know what it's like to be human. How God accomplished that spectacular birth in Bethlehem is really not that important. We do not prove that Jesus was God by the way he was conceived and born. The magnificent thing we rejoice in is the fact that he died on the cross for us sinners and came out of the grave.

| Virgin birth |

We mention Pontius Pilate in our creed simply to say we believe this was an actual time in history, during the reign of a certain Roman governor, that Jesus lived.

We believe, we say in this part of the creed, that Jesus died on the cross for our forgiveness. Notice that he didn't do it because we were so great or we deserved it, but simply because this

| Forgiveness |

is the way God loves. He takes our sin upon himself on that cross, and thus we have forgiveness even though we haven't deserved it. That cross is still the great symbol of our church as we put it on the top of our church steeples, poking it up into the clouds, and wear it around our necks.

The statement that "He descended into hell" was added to the creed very late and was not apostolic. There is a lot of debate about what it means. About all we know is that it was added in order to combat a heresy that was being taught.

| Hell |

It did such a good job we now don't know what that heresy was. It would probably be better to translate it this way: "He went to the place of the dead."

We Lutheran Christians hold that this statement probably means, as stated in 2 Peter, that once Jesus had died on the cross, he went into the very depths of hell to proclaim his victory over the power that works against God and over death itself. We see this as the first state of exultation of our Christ as he proclaims his victory over his enemies in triumph. The Reformed denominations would see this "descended into hell" more as a description of what a terrible time it was when Jesus took the sins of the world upon himself as he died. They would say it meant his crucifixion was very hellish. We can accept that also.

We do believe that Jesus actually died and went through all the pain any human would go through in a crucifixion. We believe he was completely dead, all of him, and then on Easter morning he came out of the grave through a resurrection. This is very important to us because we also believe that, because we are

| Resurrection |

baptized into a union with him, when we die we also have the privilege of coming out of the grave as he did.

This part of the creed goes on to say that we believe that God now is one and Jesus is, indeed, a part of that oneness. It states, too, that we believe he will come again. Many Christians would believe, as I do, that that "coming

| Coming again |

again" has already taken place when he came to us in Spirit.

Others would hold that this "coming again" would be a particular time in history that we can anticipate in the future.

Still others (and I like this idea too) would believe that this "coming again" happens at the time of our death.

The third article of the creed is called "Sanctification," and it's about the Holy Spirit.

The Holy Spirit is simply a name for God's presence with us in the here-and-now. After he

| Third article |

created us and after he saved us, we believe that, rather than leave us alone to struggle by ourselves, he arranged to be with us in Spirit.

Never alone

This means that no Christian ever has to face anything alone. The very one who is the Almighty, the creator of all things, and the genesis of all there is; the one, who came in person and saw that we have forgiveness and then came out of the grave to see that we have eternity, is the same one who is with us in spirit right here in this life as well as the life to come.

When we mention the "holy catholic church," we don't mean a particular denomination, but just that we are a part of one universal church of Jesus Christ around the world. The "fellowship of the saints" is a description of what the church

Catholic

is in the world. It is God's family when we get together. We come together to celebrate, to give encouragement to each other, to worship and praise God, and to accept the means of grace which are baptism and communion.

That fellowship is very precious and important to us, and we enjoy it and are sustained by it on a daily basis.

The "forgiveness of sins" is the belief that we do not have to make it on our own in order to be saved. It says that God arranged to take our wickedness upon himself and to give us his good- ness. This makes us "savable." It's the reason we call Friday of Holy Week "Good Friday." We are the forgiven of God.

Forgiveness of sins

The "resurrection of the body" means that, at the time we die we are dead, but we do not stay dead. We believe that, as Christ did, we will have a resurrection. In the 15th chapter of 1 Cor-

Resurrection

inthians Paul tells us that we will have given to a us a new body, not made with earthly hands. So, even as Christ came out of the grave on that first Easter, we anticipate coming out of the grave and having our own Easter experience after we die. In a great sense, we are the Easter and resurrection people.

Easter people

To say in this creed that we believe in "life everlasting" is to say that there is something beyond our death and the grave. Perhaps the

Life everlasting

best definition of hell is simply to say that it means to be left alone by our own choice. Perhaps the best definition of heaven is to say we are now with God. We see in the future the possibility of being with all of God's people and with the creator himself in a beautiful and new relationship.

We Christians also believe that our heaven or hell can begin here while we are still in this body and alive here on earth. We believe that once we are joined with Christ in our baptism, nothing can separate us from that union unless we just outright reject it. For that reason, we live in two kingdoms: the kingdom of the present world and the kingdom of the next world.

Two kingdoms:

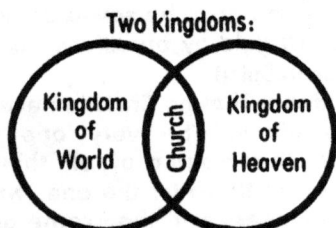

Kingdom of World — Church — Kingdom of Heaven

We have looked at the three ecumenical creeds of the church. We wanted to see that there are certain very old and formal statements of Christianity that reflect what Christians have believed right down from the very first Pentecost experience and birthday of the church. Of course, we do not worship the creed. We do worship that which it reflects in the words which have spoken for so many down through the years of Christianity.

These creeds are not prayers; but rather, they are statements of how we view God and how people have viewed God all down through the centuries. We say them when we get together to reflect those things on which we are united and hold in common.

> Statement of belief

We could certainly worship without any of these creeds, but they are an aid in our common statement of what we believe.

With our look at the creeds, we come to the end of this six-part booklet of "Lutheran Christians and Their Beliefs." There are many other things to learn about Christians in general and Lutherans in particular. We tried to include in this printing those things which are most crucial for understanding us and our beliefs.

> Summary

If, after reading this material, you are interested in becoming a part of a Lutheran congregation, the following four methods are the ways in which people join Lutheran churches:

> How to join

Baptism: If you have never been baptized, become a member of the church of Jesus Christ and of a particular Lutheran church by being baptized.

Confirmation: If you have been baptized, but never affirmed that baptism as an adult Christian, join us by attending the pastor's information class and then receiving the rite of Affirmation of Baptism.

Transfer: If you are already an active adult member of a Christian congregation, join by transfer to a particular Lutheran church.

Affirmation of Faith: If you are in any other category than above, take the pastor's information class and then join by Affirmation of Faith. This is usually for Christians who have drifted away from the congregation and allowed their membership to go on the "inactive status."

A quick look in the Yellow Pages of the phone book will locate the Lutheran church in your area.

I am quite confident that a Lutheran pastor in any community would be very willing to discuss further with you our approach to believing in and worshipping Jesus Christ, our Savior.

www.ingramcontent.com/pod-product-compliance
Lightning Source LLC
Chambersburg PA
CBHW071105040426
42443CB00008B/966